MANDEE,

NOTHING

ALL MY BEST,

ANDY

OUT OF REACH BUT IN SIGHT

ISBN: 1493739980
ISBN 13: 9781493739981
Library of Congress Control Number: 2013921598
LCCN Imprint Name: CreateSpace Independent Publishing Platform,
North Charleston, South Carolina

OUT OF REACH BUT IN SIGHT

Using Goals to Achieve Your Impossible

—

ANDREW LACIVITA

To the Evans Scholars: impossible is an opinion—
one that will never be shared by me.

Contents

A goal is nothing more than a vehicle to enhance your enjoyment of something you love. If it doesn't do that, it's not worth setting.

Goals should be set for things you love. The single greatest reason people fail at their goals is because they set them for something they don't love.

Goals can be set for anything in your life, but there are basically two ways to look at them. You can focus on the process or the outcome.

Go big. Aim high. After all, the goal is there to enrich your life, not to serve as a judgment.

You need a map. It serves as a guide that helps you stay on track. It keeps you from meandering and also shows how far you've come and how far you still need to go.

At the end of your journey, as you write your life's story, make absolutely sure that nowhere along the way do you hand the pen to someone else.

About the Author

A nationally recognized recruitment consultant, author, and inspirational speaker, Andrew LaCivita is the founder and chief executive officer of milewalk, a prominent Chicago-based executive search firm.

Throughout his career, he has helped more than one hundred and fifty companies improve their business processes, technology solutions, and employment resources. He became a trusted media resource after the inauguration of his books and motivational speaking, appearing on many television and radio shows.

Andrew is also the author of *Interview Intervention: Communication That Gets You Hired,* the first in a series of milewalk business books designed to help individuals secure the right job and organizations make smart hiring decisions.

ALSO BY ANDREW LACIVITA

Interview Intervention: Communication That Gets You Hired (2012)

ACKNOWLEDGMENTS

To Mary Burns, thank you for thinking of me.

To the Western Golf Association, thank you for having me.

To the Evans Scholars, thank you for listening to me.

To Laura Wilkens, thank you for transcribing.

Impossible is just a big word thrown around by small men who find it easier to live in the world they've been given than to explore the power they have to change it. Impossible is not a fact. It's an opinion. Impossible is not a declaration. It's a dare. Impossible is potential. Impossible is temporary. Impossible is nothing.

—Muhammad Ali

INTRODUCTION

In the spring of 2013, I received an e-mail from my friend Mary Burns. Here is the unedited version:

> *I'm at the Western Golf Association Evans Scholars' office working on a project. You came to mind about a special task related to the project. It involves forty-five minutes of your time and some preparation with yours truly. Are you in town? I'd love to get you involved and will share more!*
>
> *Hugs. M.*

Mary is one of those friends you simply don't say no to, and I wasn't about to try because that would have been futile. It turned out she wanted me to be the keynote speaker at the Western Golf Association's upcoming Career and Exposition Day it hosts for the recipients of its Evans Scholarship. The headline was "Leadership for Life: Setting and Accomplishing Your Goals." Here is what I told them. It reads like I speak.

WHAT IS A GOAL?

Welcome, everyone. My name is Andy LaCivita, and I will introduce myself a bit more as we get into the speech. You'll hear about what I do professionally and some of my hobbies through the stories I'll share, so I don't want to spend a lot of time upfront doing that.

I do want to thank all of you for taking time to listen to me speak. I'm really excited about what I'm about to share. I know everything you do in life is a choice. You had a choice to come today, and I'm glad you did. I also want to give a big thank-you to the team that pulled this together. It's very humbling when people ask you to speak to a large body because they think you have something to offer. I want to thank the entire committee and everyone involved. I think you pulled together a great program. I really mean it.

That committee actually gave me a headline of what they wanted me to share. It was "Leadership for Life: Setting and Accomplishing Your Goals." Oftentimes when I get a headline or topic or whatever it might be that someone wants me to speak about, I have an initial reaction about what to share. I did in this case too. My first thought was, *This is going to be fantastic! I can finally share all the great tools and techniques I've developed throughout my life that aided me in my accomplishments.* I've done a lot of different things. I've tried a lot of different techniques. I thought this would be a great opportunity to share all of this with you.

Then I thought, *Well, I've used different techniques at different times in my life, and I've used different techniques to accomplish my goals, depending on the particular goal.* I also thought about the audience and how many of you would be here today—three hundred or some odd number. Then I thought, *There are probably three hundred good techniques to accomplish goals, so this is going to be tricky. How am I going to do this? How am I going to package this? Huh. Maybe this isn't such a great idea.* Then I decided I didn't want to talk about that.

Then I thought about where you are in your lives. You're in school—academics! You're taking classes. You're learning subjects you're hopefully enjoying. You're going to graduate soon. Maybe I should talk about all the really, really slick techniques I used to accomplish my academic goals.

Then I thought, *Well, most of them are only in school for four years. That's a pretty short amount of time. Some of them are already almost finished. Anything I share with them regarding school and academics is going to be relatively short-lived, at least from a value standpoint.* I didn't think you'd get much out of that, so I'm not going to speak about that either.

Now I was really scratching my head and thinking I didn't have much left to talk about. I wasn't really sure what to say!

—

Asking the right questions throughout your life will do far more for you than when you think you know all the answers.

—

Whenever I get into those situations, I ask myself a question. It's usually something such as, "If I were them, what would I want to know? What could I have told my younger self that would have had the most profound impact on the way I lived the next twenty-five years of my life? If people had sat down with me at that time in my life, what could they have told me that would have shaped my life in a positive way? What would that have been? What would have had the greatest impact?"

Then it came to me. I knew what I would have told my younger self. I knew what I wanted to know then. So I asked myself that question. I can tell you this—asking the right questions throughout your life will do far more for you than when you think you know all the answers.

So I did. I had the ultimate question: "What would I have wanted to know?" Now I just needed to think about what I wanted to say. I had *the* centerpiece around which to build this talk. I was going to use it as my guideline. If anything I imagined did not answer that question, it did not make this speech. So that's it. That's what we are going to do. I figured it out. I was inspired. I actually figured it out in my sleep. I'm going to share that with you in a few minutes.

Speaking of questions, I have a few for you before I tell you how I got there: *Why do we live? What do we live for? Why do you live?* I don't want you to answer just yet. It's a simple question. I don't want a paragraph. I want a sentence or two. I want you to park that question in your mind. We will come back to it in a few minutes.

—

Dreams are not only for

dreaming...

—

Let's go back to how I arrived at what we're going to talk about. It was a Wednesday during the last week of June. It was late in the evening. I hadn't yet conceptualized what I wanted to say. I knew what I didn't want to say. I had the question I'd ask myself as the basis for this talk, but I didn't have the answer. Like a lot of people, when you have something on your mind and you go to sleep, you tend to dream about it. I did. I had a dream, and I'm going to tell you about it.

Before I tell you the dream, I'd like to explain what I do professionally so the dream makes sense. I'm a professional recruiter. I founded a recruitment firm approximately ten years ago called milewalk. Just like the name sounds, I walked a mile in your shoes. To explain at a very high level, companies large and small need to find employees to work at their companies. They need to find people for jobs. Most companies are not equipped to find all the employees they need to make their companies work effectively. Sometimes they encounter situations where they either need a lot of people or they need a person with a very unique skillset. To help them find the right people, they engage a professional recruitment firm to recruit those individuals on their behalf. That's what we do. We help companies find people for their jobs.

We also get to work with the employees. We find them. We interview them. We evaluate them to see if they and the companies are a good fit for one another. That's one of the best parts about what we do—helping both parties improve themselves. It's fantastic, and I really enjoy it.

Now let's get back to my dream. I went to sleep and found myself in the house I grew up as a child. My parents lived in this particular house for more than twenty years. It was a fantastic house filled with lots of love. There was Mom, Dad, and me, and then came along my two sisters and brother. Even my grandmother lived with us for a long time. We had a dining room and living room that were right next to each other. They formed a really big great room. We had big parties there.

I was in the dream. I was standing in the dining room. Sitting at the dining room table were a bunch of people. I noticed at one end of the table was the big boss from one of the companies we were representing (hiring on behalf of). Around the rest of the table were people he worked with. All of these people were my clients. At the other end of the table was my job candidate. This was the potential employee we recruited. We were trying to get the two of them to join each other. They were talking. I couldn't really make out what they were saying. You know how dreams are.

In walked my mother. She came from the kitchen, which was next to the dining room. She was carrying two big volumes—scrapbooks she had prepared for me as a gift for my fortieth birthday a few years ago. OK, it was seven years ago. This part is actually real. The two big volumes were in her hands. They covered the first twenty years and the second twenty years. There they were in all their glory. In them were pictures of everything you could imagine from my life. I was born. There were pictures. I went to kindergarten. There were pictures. There was football, baseball, eighth-grade graduation, high school, college, jobs, and the companies I started. There were more pictures. It was the most amazing gift I've ever gotten in my life.

She decided she wanted to show everybody these books. She started to tap my clients on the shoulders. I thought, *Oh no! Mom! Please. No. No.* It didn't matter. She gave me the big wave of her hand that said, "Andrew, I'm your mother. I get to do whatever I want. I'm showing these pictures." I was thinking, *Please, not the ones with the bad hair and the braces too!*

Around the table she went. She tapped everyone on the shoulder. She flipped through the books. Finally, when she was done, she left. They all got up. They started to move toward the door. I raced over. I wanted to shake everybody's hand on the way out. The big boss was last.

I asked, "Well, how'd it go?"

He replied, "We liked your guy. We want to hire him."

"That's great!"

"Yeah, that's not even the best part."

"What's the best part?" I asked.

"We all really loved getting to see the pictures of your life," he answered.

"Why's that?"

"Because that is what life is all about. What you do every day matters far more than what you do once in a while."

—

*What you do every day matters
far more than what you do once
in a while.*

—

It's the day to day. It's not so much the major milestones that really make you. It's like that in everything, from your relationships to school to work. Straight As do not happen because you're a whiz. They require smart studying or perhaps efficient studying. They require analysis and evaluation and so on and so forth. Promotions at work do not happen because you completed one project successfully. Smart, hard work every day is what matters.

I want to have a discussion with you centered on getting everything you want out of your life and having fun doing it. I want it to transcend time. I don't care how old you are. Anybody in the audience can enjoy this. It doesn't matter where you are. You are never too late in your life to become the person you are capable of being. I don't care if you're a boy, a girl, a husband, or a wife. This will be ageless and timeless. It doesn't matter what your profession is or what you're studying in school. It doesn't matter whether you go to work on a baseball field or in a restaurant or in a skyscraper. The concepts I will share will transcend all of that. None of those things will make any difference with what I'm about to tell you.

Now I want to go back to the question. Why do we live?

—

Why I live...

—

Well, I'll tell you what I live for. I have two goals. They're so simple I don't have to write them down. The first one is I want to be happy. I want to have fun in my life. I know what makes me happy, but I've also done quite a bit of soul searching. That's number one.

The second is I want to make you the best you *you* can be. I don't want to help make you the you he thinks you should be or she thinks you should be or your parents think you should be or your teachers think you should be or, even worse, society thinks you should be—just the best you *you* want to be. Nobody can be better at being you than you, so I want to make you the best you.

For me, that goes for everyone who passes me in life. I want to make others better for having met me. I also want to reach out to people I've not yet met and make them better. That's what I'm working on now. So there you have my two goals.

—

A goal is nothing more than a vehicle to enhance your enjoyment of something you love. The actual attainment of the goal is far less important than the positive impact working toward that goal has on your life.

—

There are two more things I want to tell you. They are probably the most important things I'm going to say in the next half hour. If you don't remember anything I say for the next half hour except these two things, you'll be able to figure the rest of life out. Just remember these two things. I'll say them a few times because they are a central theme.

N-u-m-b-e-r one—the most important thing I'm going to say: a goal, to me, is nothing more than a vehicle to enhance your enjoyment of something you love. If it doesn't do that, it's not worth setting.

Number two—the second most important thing I'm going to say: the actual attainment of the goal is far less important than the positive impact working toward that goal will have on your life.

If you can keep those two thoughts in mind, you'll be OK. I think you'll get what you want out of life if you look at things that way.

Now that you understand what a goal is, we're going to talk about four things related to goals. First, I'll help you identify them and understand where they come from. Second, I'll give you a perspective—albeit my perspective—on how to look at them based on the types of goals that exist. Third, I'll help you understand how to set a goal. Fourth, I'll provide a formula to achieve your goals. I'll give you something you can apply across any goal.

Where Do Goals Come From?

I love questions. Here's one for you: Where do goals come from? In fact, the better question might be, "Where *should* they come from?"

Let's pause for a second. In my job as a recruiter, I interview a lot of people. My team and I continually evaluate people to see if they're a good fit for the organizations we represent.

In my lifetime—I'm not kidding—I've interviewed more than ten thousand people. To put that in perspective, that's well more than thirty times the number of people in this room. That's a lot of evaluation. That's a lot of data. I'm big on statistics. During the course of my career, I've reviewed loads of statistics, and I've identified three things all successful people have in common. I'm talking about people who live the most enriched lives— not riches but enriched lives. They're happy and fulfilled. Some might even call them lucky. Whatever you call them, they have three things in common—passion, vision, and commitment.

—

All successful people have three things in common—passion, vision, and commitment.

—

Notice I didn't use words such as *intelligence, money,* or other things many people think are required to be successful. It's those three things—passion, vision, commitment. What are they?

Passion. You're not born with it. It's something you develop. It's a love for something you were exposed to from the time you were born until now. You fell in love with it. You became interested in it and then passionate about it. You genuinely love it.

Vision. It's your ability to see where you want to take that love. How will you grow it? How will you nurture it? Where will it take you?

Commitment. It's your dedication to fulfilling that love.

—

The single greatest reason people fail to achieve a goal is because they set the goal for something they didn't truly love. Only set big goals for something you love.

—

Before we get to the answer regarding where goals should come from, I want to share with you why people don't achieve their goals. There are certainly many reasons why people fail. There's bad setting, bad planning, and bad execution. There's bad this and bad that. There are loads of reasons.

The single greatest reason people don't achieve their goals is because the goals were set for something they didn't love. When you set them for things you don't love, you don't work as hard at them. They're not as important to you. Sometimes you just want to get through things.

I want to go back to what I said earlier. Goals exist to enhance your enjoyment of the things you love, so you should set them regarding things you love. There you have it. Set them for things you love!

—

If my life is the only life that's changed as a result of my accomplishing this, is that good enough for me?

—

At the end of each of these sections, I have some quotes or affirmations. I've developed them over time for me. I use them often. Please use them if you feel they'll help.

Whenever I'm about to undertake something, I ask myself one question before I take the first step—*before* I take the *first* step. I refuse to get into something and then decide later. I decide—and commit—before I take that first step.

I ask myself, if my life is the only life that's changed as a result of me accomplishing this, is that good enough for me? If my life is the only life that's changed as a result of me attempting it, accomplishing it, doing it, or whatever, is that good enough for me?

If the answer is yes, I do it. If the answer is no, then I take myself through this complicated maze of a variety of questions to determine whether I'm going to do it. The answer in 99 percent of those cases is no. That's never the case, however, when I set the goal for something I love.

THE TYPES OF GOALS

I titled this section of the talk the types of goals, but I believe that is a bit of a misnomer. It's probably not the correct title. This part is really more of a philosophy of how I look at goals.

What's going to happen, I guarantee you, is throughout your life people will approach you or you will approach them to set goals—financial goals, relationship goals, health goals, athletic goals, professional goals, so forth and so on. You name it. Anything you can imagine, somebody is going to want you to set a goal for it.

I don't look at my goals that way or in those categories. I look at them in two forms. I call them outcome goals and process goals. They are just like they sound.

—

Set goals for anything you want, but there are really only two types—outcome and process. Process people live happier lives.

—

For outcome goals, you target something very specific, as in a particular result. It's a number, timeframe, or dollar amount. They're usually something of that nature. Oftentimes with outcome goals where you're trying to achieve something very specific, you rely on elements outside your control. These elements can be things such as the stock markets, weather, other people, and so on—elements you can do nothing to control.

Process goals, on the other hand, are usually about you enjoying the journey. They tend to be goals wrapped inside a plan you're using to achieve an even bigger goal. And one goal is usually simply working the plan effectively. These goals are also typically 100 percent within your control. They are, by design, entirely up to you.

Now, goal gurus—people who speak about goals, write about goals, and help facilitate achieving your goals—often preach setting very specific goals. Their theory is by shooting for a specific target, you substantially increase your odds of achieving the goal. In essence, you need to know where you're going to get there.

I agree with specificity but only as it relates to process as opposed to outcome. I think you need to be very specific about the plans you prepare to achieve the goal. If you're *too* focused on the outcome or hitting it, you often lose sight of what you're doing at any moment. Those moments along the way are your stepping stones toward that outcome.

Let me give you an example. I'm a marathon runner. I love to run. Here are a couple different perspectives. One is the outcome perspective, and the other is a process perspective.

The outcome person says, "I'm going to run a marathon in three hours. I'll make T-shirts that say three hours. I'll write the number three everywhere—in my books, on my desk, on my refrigerator. It's three hours or bust. I'm going to go through my training plan. I'm going to run hard, and I'm going to log my miles so I can get to that running pace that helps me finish within three hours."

The process person says, "I want to run a marathon. I'm going to research it. I'm going to develop a sound training plan. I'll make that plan my first goal. I'm going to work each training run—hill runs, tempo runs, speed work, long runs, and so forth. I'll make that my second goal. I'm going to listen to my body. If my body tells me it's sore, I'll dial it back. I'll evaluate myself on how effectively I respond to that. That will be another goal.

If I hit all those goals, then six months from now on race day, when I can't predict the weather, on a course I've never run before, with no idea of how my body will feel, I should be able run the best race I can on *that* day. On top of that, I'll take all the experience and outcome from that race and channel it into my next attempt. Most importantly, no matter what the conditions or outcome, I'm going to be happy if I finish upright and uninjured, with a smile on my face." That's the process person. These people are all about the journey.

Outcome people tend to focus on numbers. They tend to focus on the result of the race. "What was my time? What's the score at the end of the game? How quickly did I earn one hundred thousand dollars annually? What's my title at work? Why am I not this yet? Why am I not that yet?"

Process people tend to enjoy the journey. "I'll take the correct steps, and the outcome will just happen."

There is one other major difference. It relates, in general, to their happiness levels. If you often rely on elements outside your control, as outcome people often do, and these elements don't break in your favor, you run a great risk of being disappointed. You could be unhappy.

Process people don't usually look at the world that way. They focus on the process, method, and practice, take what's given to them on game day, and make the best of it.

Keep in mind the point I made earlier. It matters more what you do every day than what you do once in a while. The actual achievement or attainment of the goal is not nearly as important as the positive impact working toward that goal has on your life. Focus on that.

When I set my goals, I often target some outcome. I like to put a flag in the ground and shoot for it. However, if that undertaking is new for me, I give myself wiggle room. I'll give that target a range rather than a specific number. If I'm more experienced, I'll tighten that range. I might even be able to give it a specific number. But I only do that for things for which I'm very experienced.

—

*My mind is open to any
possibility, but my heart is
attached to no outcome.*

—

Here is another quote to close up this section. I developed it, and I hope you'll use it. I remind myself of this to keep me happy. It keeps me from getting upset when things don't go the way I thought they should.

My mind is open to any possibility, but my heart is attached to no outcome.

That doesn't mean I don't care. That means I am not going to get upset or unhappy if something doesn't break the way I thought it should. Oftentimes when you set your target, you don't have all the information you need to effectively designate that target. You often simply guess at the outcome. I never want to guess about things that are important to me.

HOW TO SET GOALS

Let's talk about how to set your goals. When I set my goals, I only think of two words: go big! Think big. If you can imagine it, it can be done. It might take some time, but it can be done.

I was half your age when I learned that concept. I learned it from fish. You guessed it—here comes a fish story. I was ten years old, and I had a friend whose name was John. He's still a friend. John was the kid down the block. He had everything—the newest video games, newest pinball machines, board games. You name it, he had it. He also had this big fish tank that I loved.

~

You can learn a lot from fish.

~

One day I came home from John's house and said, "Mom, John has a fish tank. I want a fish tank."

She said, "OK, get your shoes on. Let's go to the pet store."

Off to the pet store we went. We got there, and I said, "Mom, look at this! It's a ten-gallon tank. I'm ten years old. I want the ten-gallon tank."

She said, "You know what? We'll buy this one. It's a perfect size to put on your dresser in your bedroom. That way, in the morning when you get up, you can feed the fish. At night, you can feed the fish before you say good night."

A couple of years later, the fish died. I realized the fish had grown to be a couple of inches long. Now I was a little older, perhaps twelve or thirteen years old. I said, "Mom, I want more fish. This time I want a bigger tank."

Mom said, "OK, you're a little older now. You have your allowance money."

Back to the pet store we went. We walked in, and I asked the pet store manager, "What's the next-biggest tank size?"

He said, "It's twenty-nine gallons."

Mom said, "Wow, that's pretty big, but OK. You know what? We'll put that one in the basement. We have more room down there."

We bought more fish. They were the same kind of fish I had when I was ten years old. We brought the fish back, assembled the tank, and put the fish in. A few years later, those fish died. This time, I realized those fish grew to be two times the size of the first fish I had.

At this point, I was in my middle teenage years or so. I had a job bagging groceries at Jewel Food Store. I said, "Mom, I want a big tank now. I have money in my pocket."

Mom said, "Great. We'll take some of that money to the pet store, and we'll buy another tank."

Off to the pet store we went to buy a fifty-five-gallon tank. She looked at the tank and said, "Oh my! Let's put this tank in the living room. It'll be like a piece of furniture. Everyone can enjoy it, but you need to make sure to keep it clean."

I bought the fish—the exact same kind of fish I'd bought the last two times. I put them in the tank. I noticed that after a few years, those fish grew to be four times the size of the first fish I bought when I was ten years old. I asked, "Mom, why is it that these fish—the same kind of fish we've fed the same food to every day grew to be four times the size of the first fish we bought?"

Mom said, "Well, that's probably because things have a way of growing to the size of their environment."

I asked, "Really? Does it work like that for everything?"

She said, "Pretty much."

—

Your accomplishments in life will be in direct proportion to the height of the goals you set. Neither successes nor failures exist.

—

You need to understand that your accomplishments—your achievements in life—will be in direct proportion to the height of the goals you set. Notice I used the words *accomplishments* and *achievements*. I didn't use words like *successes* and *failures*. I know those words exist in somebody's dictionary somewhere. I don't use them. I don't think there is any such thing as success or failure. I really don't. That might sound crazy to you. There are just outcomes or results. You do something, and something happens. Whether you thought it was going to happen a certain way or whether you wanted it to happen a certain way is irrelevant.

The only difference between what somebody considered a success for that outcome and what somebody else considered a failure is perspective. It's the only difference—perspective. And the only person's perspective that matters is yours. It's yours!

Let me give you an example using another running analogy. Let's say someone wants to run her first race. She targets a 5K race. That's five kilometers or a little over three miles. She trains. She runs. She's standing upright at the end. She runs a good time. Check! That's success by somebody's definition—hers, probably.

She thinks, *Well, I'm getting this running thing down. Now I'm a little more experienced. I think I'll run another race, and this time it'll be farther. I'm going to go for the 10K or maybe the ten-miler. Wait. How about a half-marathon? Why not a full marathon? That's 26.2 miles. I'll train for that, and I'll run it!*

Now comes race day. She's at the starting line. Off she goes, but at mile twenty, she conks out. This actually happens quite a bit. Those last six to eight miles are killers. Anyone who has ever run a marathon can attest to that. She goes to the medical tent, and she's sitting there with a swollen foot. Would you say she failed? I don't know. I would say she just ran more than six times farther than she ran in her previous race. I call that raging progress. Just because she didn't finish the race doesn't mean anything—at least not anything important. I'm sure she's disappointed, but it's in the way that you look at it. It's perspective.

Here's another thing, and it's a big one. Remember, the goal is a vehicle to enhance your enjoyment of something you love. It is not there to serve as a judgment. Don't judge yourself by the outcome. Let it enrich your life, not sit as your judge.

Let's get back to setting your goals. The best point I can make is to set them high. Set them as high as you can. Set them based on your imagination. If you can imagine it, it can be done. Sure, I want you to check the outside world for sanity's sake. We want to be somewhat realistic. But keep in mind, other people's opinions of what you can and cannot accomplish—or even worse society's opinion of what you can and cannot accomplish or what can or cannot be done—are simply others projecting their limited thinking onto you. It's their limited thinking.

You should believe in yourself. Give it a try. If it doesn't work out as you thought it would, learn from it. If you try it again, you will be that much more intelligent regarding what you need to do. I guarantee what you accomplish will be in proportion to the height of the goal you set.

—

Cowards and true potential will never meet.

—

To wrap up this section, I have a couple of quotes for you. I say this first one to myself whenever I'm about to undertake something significant. It's reinforcement for me regarding where I should set the bar on a goal.

Comfort has a way of turning you into a coward, especially when you are staring at your own true potential.

This quote helps remind me that people have a way of becoming complacent with what they have. Please don't misunderstand—complacency is certainly OK if it's your life. The beauty of this world is that we all get to live the lives we want— however we want. For me, that's not OK. I'm much happier when I'm doing more things and doing them to a greater extent. I enjoy pushing myself for the things I love and for the things that matter to me. If something doesn't matter to you, then don't worry about it.

~

Most people don't aim too high and miss. Most aim too low and hit.

~

The second quote is more of an observation regarding what I see in many people.

Most people don't aim too high and miss. Most aim too low and hit.

Here is one of the few times I'll use the word *failure* to illustrate a point. To me, shooting too low is a bigger sin or failure than not hitting a goal that was set high. Many of you can achieve great heights for things you're passionate about. Shoot high. It's OK if you miss.

How to Achieve Goals

Let's do a little recap. You're going to set goals for things you love. You have insight into a good perspective regarding how to look at them, making sure you enjoy the journey toward achieving them. And you want to set the bar high. So how do we bring it all together? How do we make the best attempt toward achieving these great heights for the things we love? What do we need?

—

You need a map. The weather forecast would be nice too.

—

You need a map. You need a plan. For most of you, up to this point in your life, someone else has put the map together for you. It's been a boss, a coach, a teacher, or your parents.

What is the first thing the teacher hands you when you go into class? When you walk into the classroom on the first day—or perhaps they place it out on the Internet—what do they hand you? There it is—the syllabus—classes one through forty-eight in all their glory. There is every topic we're going to cover for the next sixteen weeks. There it is. Why? Because the teacher knows, "For me to do my job, for us to hit our goals for this class, and for my students to learn what they need to know, we need to go through all this stuff." The teacher's not going to roll out of bed on week fifteen and say, "Huh. What do I feel like teaching today?" No! There needs to be a plan—a map! And the teacher just gave it to you!

When you get out of school, the fun really starts because you get to play Magellan yourself. You get to build your own map. If you don't know who Magellan is, then you need to go take a history class. That map you build will serve as your guide.

I don't want just the map. I'd like to know the weather too. I'd love to have the map and the weather. But unfortunately, you're not going to have the weather. You're not going to see the storms coming. You're not going to see the curveballs and the sliders people are throwing at your head. Here's the bad part: the further away your goal is from today, the more storms you'll encounter. Here's the worst part: the further away your goal is from today, the greater the likelihood that somewhere along that way, you're going to fall out of love with that goal. Why?

Why do we fall out of love with something? It isn't going well! Does this sound familiar? "I'm tired. I can't remember why I loved this in the first place. I've been at this for so long. I don't even know why I got started." You are going to feel that way, so I'd like to help you avoid that. The map does that. The map is there so when your life gets interrupted and things aren't going well, it shows you how to get back on track. The map shows you how to make the adjustments to get back on track.

The map also shows you how far you've come. "Whoa—I've already gone fifty miles! I only have ten more to go!" Seeing progress nurtures your psyche. It nourishes it. It helps you build self-esteem. That nurtured psyche helps you weather the emotional and mental storms. When you get fatigued and want to throw in the towel, you can look at the map to see how far you've progressed. It helps you remember why you started in the first place.

Another great attribute of the map—or you all have those Garmins or GPS devices—is it gives you the fastest route. It'll give you an alternate route if you need one. It helps you get there as fast as possible.

—

*It's never too late or too early
to become the person you are
capable of being.*

—

I have a story for you. I consider this to be the best story I could come up with to illustrate a long-term, difficult goal. It also happens to be a golf story, which I thought was a little on the nose considering why we're here today. This story also falls under the category of it's never too late or too early to become the person you are capable of being. It's never too late if you're still breathing.

I came to golf late in life—much later than any of you. I know many of you play and some of you don't. I was thirty years old when I started playing. I didn't have any coaching or take any lessons when I started. I played for seven years, and I tried to play as well as I could by mimicking some of the great professional players. I read the golf books and magazines. I practiced hitting golf balls.

When I was thirty-seven or so, approximately ten years ago, I decided to commit myself to becoming the best player I could possibly be. I wondered how good I could become if I had proper instruction and commitment to the game. I also thought becoming a better player would enhance my enjoyment of the game.

So I went to see a coach named Kevin. I walked in on the first day, and he said, "Welcome to the program. I think you're going to like it. The first thing you need to do is hit a golf ball or two. Then we'll talk about what you'd like to get out of the program."

He hooked me up to these ridiculous contraptions and wrapped cords around my head, shoulders, and waist. There were video cameras everywhere. I hit the golf ball with a seven iron. He videotaped it. We sat down, and he said, "OK, thanks. What would you like to get out of this program?"

I said, "Kevin, it's really simple. There are only two goals I care about. I want to become a scratch golfer [zero handicap], and I want to have a lot of fun doing it."

After he picked himself up off the floor and wiped away his tears of laughter, he composed himself long enough to say, "OK, let me take another look at the video of your swing." He looked at the swing again and then looked back at me.

I asked, "Well? How long? How long before I become a scratch golfer?"

He looked at me with a stoic face and deadpanned, "Three years."

I asked, "Three years? That's a long time."

He said, "No, actually it's not. Most people are never going to achieve that, and the ones that do usually require much more time. You have a pretty decent swing, so if you work really smart and put the effort in, you can get there." Then he said, "Hit another ball."

I got the contraptions back on. I took my stance over the ball, and just as I was about to hit it, I looked up at him and asked, "When you say three years…?"

As the speech bubble was still hanging over my head, he replied, "That means every single day for the next three years, you will have a golf club in your hand doing something I have instructed you to do." I thought, *Goodness, that's something like a thousand hours or so of practice.*

I said, "This is important to me. I'll do whatever I need to, but I need a plan."

He said, "I'm going to have one for you next week."

The next week, I went back. There it was—three years of the program. The first year focused on the backswing, the second on the downswing, and the third on the short game, which included chipping, putting, and sand play.

The point is the map shows you how to get to where you're going. A long-term, multiyear plan can be very overwhelming when you don't understand where you are going. You don't become CEO of the company overnight. You don't go from a nonrunner to running a marathon in six months.

Here is another key point to remember. We spoke about setting goals very high for things you love. If they are truly, truly major goals in your life, then you can only have so many at one time. That means two or three or so. If you have too many, you'll spread yourself too thin and won't be successful in accomplishing them.

Think in terms of a pyramid or triangle. At the top, you have a few major goals in your life, and you set them very high. On the next layer, there are more short-term or intermediary goals, which are stepping stones to the top of the pyramid.

Going back to my golf example, when I returned for the second lesson, I looked at the plan Kevin had prepared, and the goal became manageable in my mind. I realized, "The first twenty weeks it'll be snowing outside. I'll be in a studio performing drills and shaping the way I think about the swing and the proper body motion. In the spring, I'll start hitting more golf balls outside at the driving range. In the summer, I'll be playing more and continually practicing. I'll work with Kevin once each month to make sure the backswing stays in order. When the summer is over, I'll go back to the studio, and I'll move onto the next phase— the downswing and so on." All of a sudden, it became easier for me to digest this lofty goal. I had a blueprint.

Here's something you need to remember about big goals. I realize everyone wants a finished product right away, but you need to be patient. You should enjoy yourself along the way. As you work toward something—and anybody who plays golf knows this—your progress will not always be linear and rising. You will have setbacks. Embrace those setbacks. You know what setbacks do? They tap you on the shoulder and say, "Hello! Take a pause and examine things. What's going wrong? Rethink things." When you take that pause and step back, you often will subsequently take a giant leap forward. The map, at this point, is extremely crucial because it keeps you from meandering and gets you back on track quickly.

Back to the golf story. After four years of this training, practicing, and playing, I reached my goal. Yes, I was a year tardy, but hey, stuff came up. Life sometimes interrupts you and takes you off your desired path and timetable. At that moment, four years later, something undetectable happened. I wasn't enjoying myself. I wasn't enjoying golf. I had never anticipated this could happen. I had just reached a pinnacle I had worked so diligently toward, and I wasn't enjoying myself anymore. I didn't know why until I realized how difficult it would be to maintain that level of proficiency. In essence, getting there as I watched myself continually improve was much more enjoyable than being there at the pinnacle and needing to stay there.

The big lesson I want you to understand is that a goal can never be an endpoint. Regardless of what goal you set or how high you set it, it should never be an endpoint. Technically it can never be an endpoint because time keeps moving. The world keeps spinning. Whatever goals you set in life, however big they are, they will always be mere stepping stones to something else. I don't know what that something else is, but whatever it is, goals will get you there.

—

There is no such thing as wasted time.

—

There's one last point I'd like to make before we wrap up this section. All the hard work you put into achieving your goals will never be wasted. It will never be lost. There is absolutely no such thing as wasted time. You will always learn something. You will be more intelligent, especially if you're paying attention and have the proper outlook, embracing the lessons. Maybe you learned you didn't like something. That's fine. Channel that lesson into becoming a more-evolved person. That newer, more evolved person will be smarter at whatever he or she attempts next.

CLOSING TIME

To close up the discussion, I'd like to review the key messages.

- Set your goals for something you love. Remember, a goal is nothing more than a vehicle to enhance your enjoyment of something you love. If it doesn't do that, it's not worth setting.
- You should have a good perspective on how to look at your goals. Get into the process and get out of the outcome.
- Set your goals high. Set them very high! Don't worry if you fall short. Set them up there as high as you can imagine.
- Develop and work your plan. Most importantly, enjoy the steps along the plan.

—

At the end of your journey, as you write your life's story, make absolutely sure that nowhere along the way do you hand the pen to someone else.

—

Now I'd like you to rush out into the world. Set whatever goals you are going to set. I hope you have them throughout your life. I hope you take steps in the right direction. But please, whatever you do, do not ignore those steps as you take them because those steps are actually your life story.

Whenever your journey ends—and hopefully that's way down the line—and you write your life's story, make sure that nowhere along the way do you hand the pen to somebody else. These are your goals. Set them for you.

Made in the USA
Charleston, SC
23 January 2014